武満 徹

チェロとピアノのための

オリオン

TORU TAKEMITSU
ORION

for cello and piano

SJ 1019

© 1984, Schott Music Co. Ltd., Tokyo
International Copyright Secured.
All Rights Reserved.

チェロとピアノのための《オリオン》は、オーストリア放送協会（ORF）の委嘱により作曲された。1984年3月21日、ウィーンで、フロリアン・キット（チェロ）とハラルド・オスバーガー（ピアノ）によって初演された。

演奏時間——12分

Orion for cello and piano was commissioned by Österreichischer Rundfunk (ORF).
The first performance was given by Florian Kitt, cello and Harald Ossberger, piano in Vienna on March 21, 1984.

Duration: 12 minutes

ABBREVIATIONS AND SYMBOLS:

For Cello:

S.P.	= sul ponticello
P.O.	= Position ordinary
♯ ♮ ♭	= 1/4 tone higher
♯ ♮ ♭	= 1/4 tone lower
o—<	= dal niente

For Piano:

pizz.	= Pluck the string directly with the finger or fingernail. (with ped.)
Mute	= Mute directly on the bottom end of the string with the finger and then play normally with the pedal.

Orion
オリオン
for cello and piano

Toru Takemitsu
武満 徹

© 1984, Schott Music Co. Ltd., Tokyo

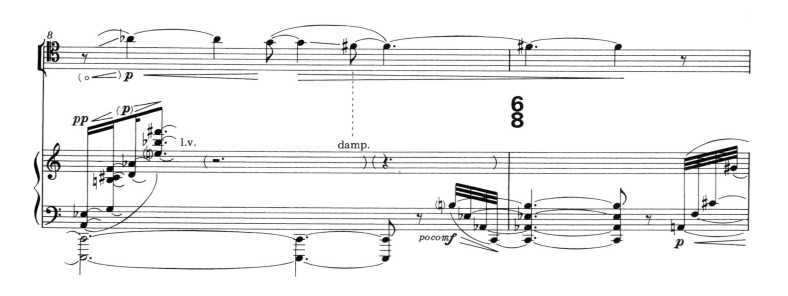

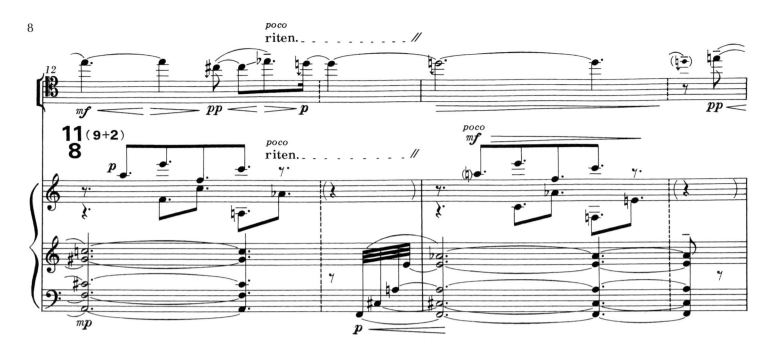

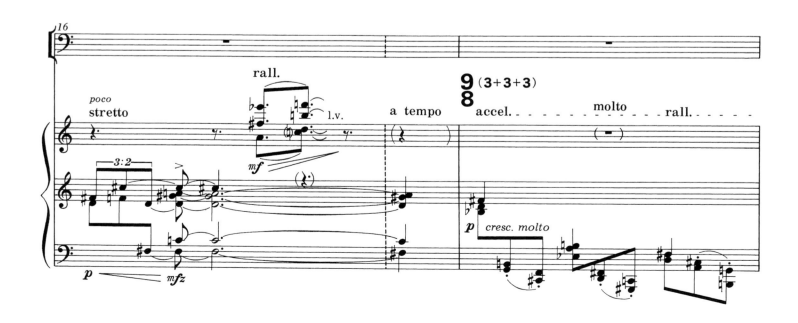

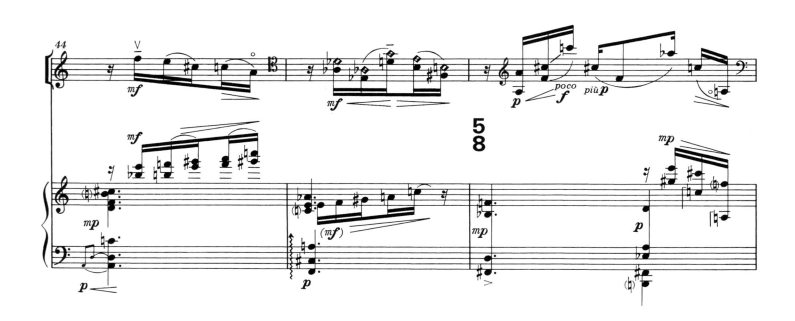

武満 徹

チェロとピアノのための

オリオン

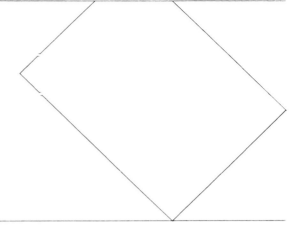

TORU TAKEMITSU
ORION

for cello and piano

SJ 1019

Cello

© 1984, Schott Music Co. Ltd., Tokyo
International Copyright Secured.
All Rights Reserved.

Cello

Orion
オリオン
for cello and piano

Toru Takemitsu
武満 徹

© 1984, Schott Music Co. Ltd., Tokyo

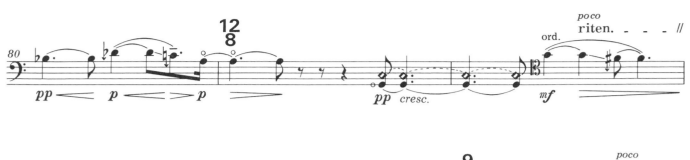
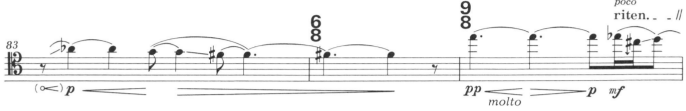

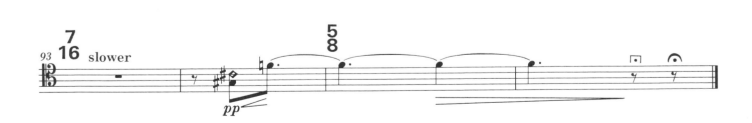

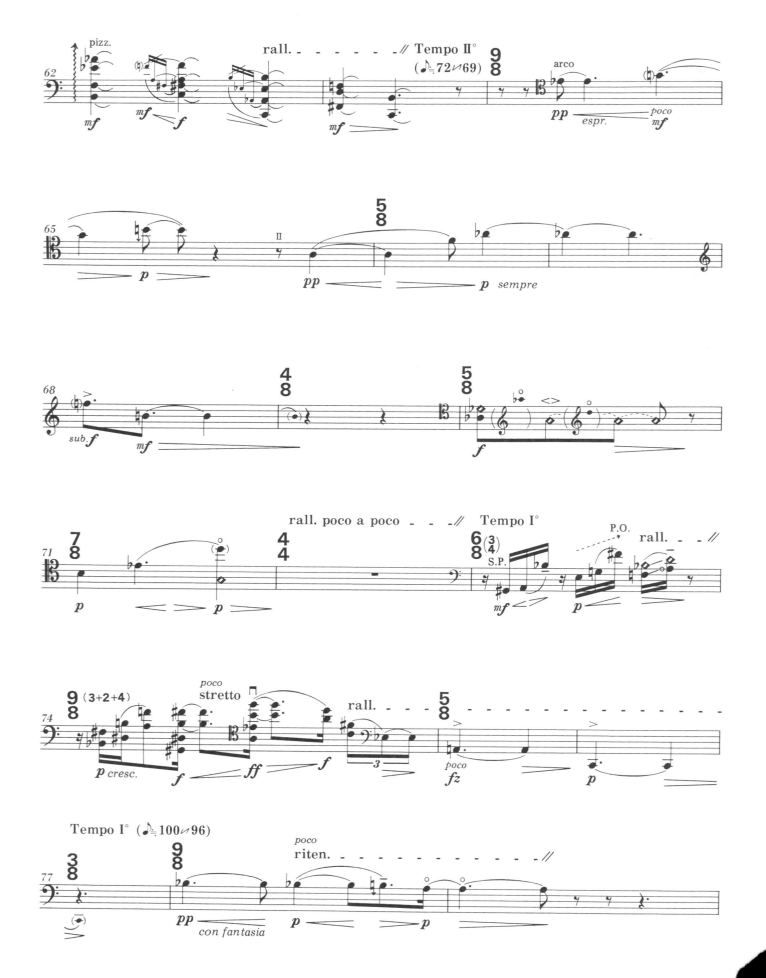

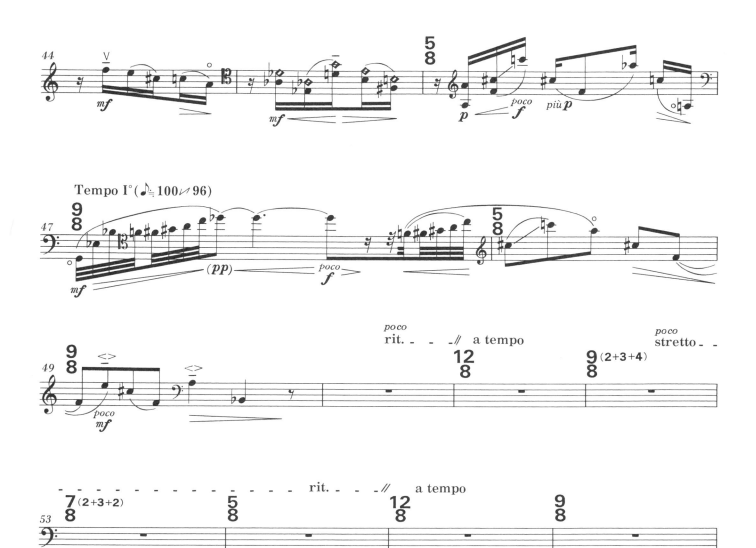

ABBREVIATIONS AND SYMBOLS:

S.P. = sul ponticello
P.O. = Position ordinary
♯ ♮ ♭ = 1/4 tone higher
♯ ♮ ♭ = 1/4 tone lower
o─< = dal niente

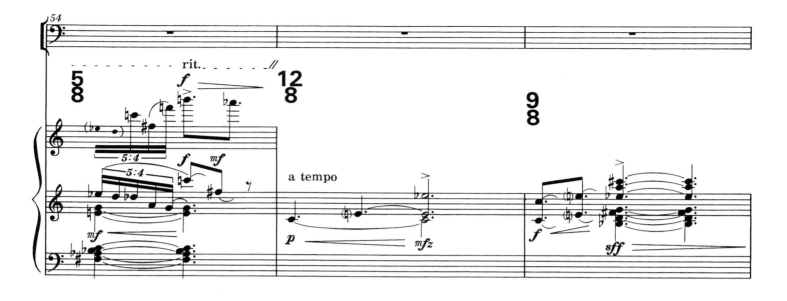

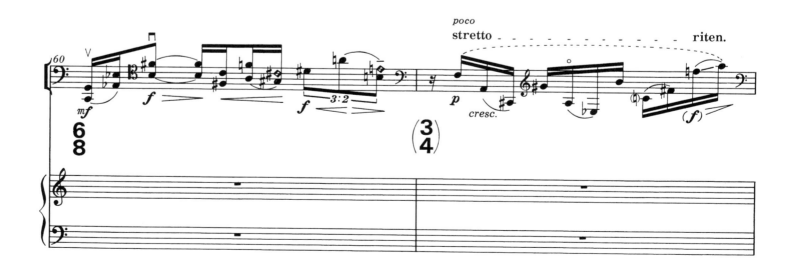

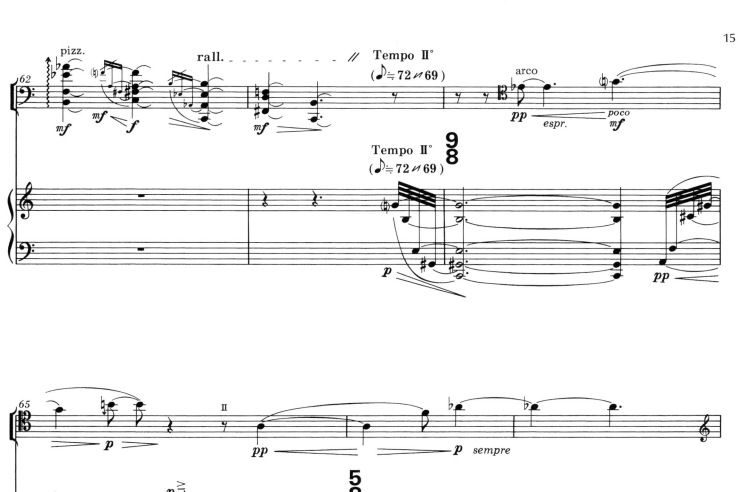
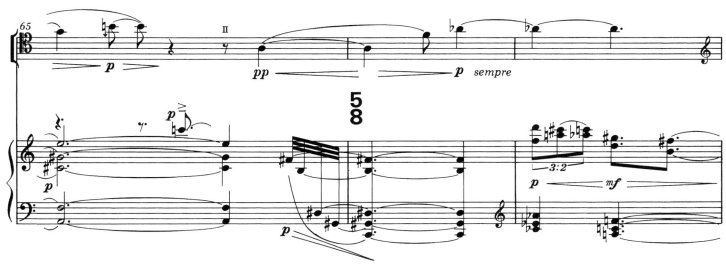
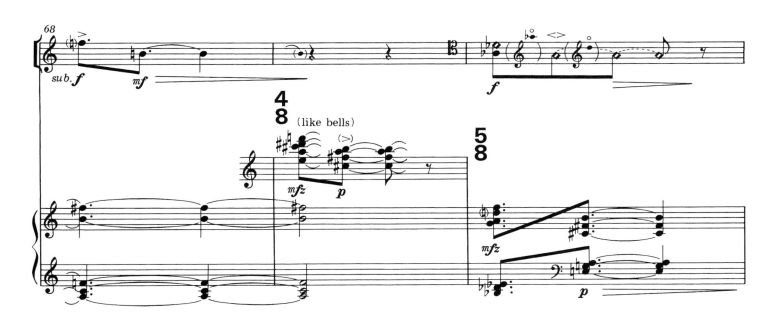

武満 徹《オリオン》	●
チェロとピアノのための	
初版発行	1984年5月25日
第4版第1刷⑥	2016年3月25日
発行	ショット・ミュージック株式会社
	東京都千代田区内神田1-10-1 平富ビル3階
	〒101-0047
	(03)6695-2450
	http://www.schottjapan.com
	ISBN 978-4-89066-319-4
	ISMN M-65001-056-6

現代の音楽
MUSIC OF OUR TIME

武満 徹　Toru Takemitsu (1930-1996)

オリオンとプレアデス
Orion and Pleiades
for cello and orchestra ... SJ 1030 ... 6400 円

シーン
Scene
for violoncello and string orchestra ... SJ 1151 ... 1200 円

ビトゥイーン・タイズ
Between Tides
for violin, cello and piano ... SJ 1091 (score & parts) ... 4800 円

妖精の距離
Distance de Fée
for violin and piano ... SJ 1050 (score & part) ... 2100 円

十一月の霧と菊の彼方から
From far beyond Chrysanthemums and November Fog
for violin and piano ... SJ 1014 (score & part) ... 2000 円

鳥が道に降りてきた
A Bird came down the Walk
for viola accompanied by piano ... SJ 1092 (score & part) ... 2100 円

一柳 慧　Toshi Ichiyanagi (1933-)

インタークロス
Intercross
for violin and piano ... SJ 1075 (performing score) ... 3500 円

コズミック・ハーモニー
Cosmic Harmony
for violoncello and piano ... SJ 1110 (performing score) ...1600 円

夏の花
Flowers Blooming in Summer
for harp and piano ... SJ 1016 (performing score) ... 1800 円

パガニーニ・パーソナル
Paganini Personal
for marimba and piano ... SJ 1013 (performing score) ... 2000 円

プラーナ
Prāṇa
for piano quintet ... SJ 1024 (performing score) ... 3500 円

リカレンス
Recurrence
for flute, clarinet, percussion, harp, piano, violin and cello ...
SJ 1020 (performing score) ... 2800 円

湯浅讓二　Joji Yuasa (1929-)

ソリテュード・イン・メモリアム T. T.
Solitude in Memoriam T.T.
for violin, violoncello and piano ... SJ 1106 (score & parts) ... 3000 円

細川俊夫　Toshio Hosokawa (1955-)

ヴァーティカル・タイム・スタディ III
Vertical Time Study III
for violin and piano ... SJ 1087 (score & part) ... 2300 円

古代の舞い
Ancient Dance
for violin and piano ... SJ 1143 (score & part) ... 2800 円

マニフェステーション
Manifestation
for violin and piano ... SJ 1120 (score & part) ... 2300 円

デュオ
Duo
for violin and violoncello ... SJ 1115 (performing score) ... 1300 円

時の深みへ
In die Tiefe der Zeit
for violoncello and accordion ... SJ 1114 (score & part) ... 2800 円

メモリー －尹伊桑の追憶に－
Memory - In Memory of Isang Yun -
for violin, violoncello and piano ... SJ 1101 (score & parts) ... 2300 円

ヴァーティカル・タイム・スタディ I
Vertical Time Study I
for clarinet, violoncello and piano ... SJ 1078 (score & parts) ... 3300 円

高橋悠治　Yuji Takahashi (1938-)

チッ(ト)
Ji(t)
for flute and piano ... SJ 1039 ... 1400 円

権代敦彦　Gondai Atsuhiko (1965-)

虹
L'arc-en-ciel
for alto saxophone and piano ... SJ 1156 (score & part) ... 3000 円

ショット・ミュージック株式会社
東京都千代田区内神田1-10-1　平富ビル3階　〒101-0047
電話 (03) 6695-2450　ファクス (03) 6695-2579
sales@schottjapan.com　http://www.schottjapan.com

SCHOTT MUSIC CO. LTD.
Hiratomi Bldg., 1-10-1 Uchikanda, Chiyoda-ku, Tokyo 101-0047
Telephone: (+81)3-6695-2450　Fax: (+81)3-6695-2579
sales@schottjapan.com　http://www.schottjapan.com

（価格には消費税が含まれておりません）